POEMS AND THOUGHTS

A BOOK BY JESSE E. REESE

Table of Contents

A Beautiful Memory

There is a flower
That beauty has found,
To hold her and kiss her
My mind goes round.
There is no match
To this beauty,
When the sun shines on her
I can barely see.
When you're not happy
And full of life,
My heart is full of pain
Like it was cut by a knife.
I know now why
I feel this way,
Feelings get stronger
Each step of the way.
Once again it's
Only a dream,
That's trapped me on
This endless stream.
I try to wake up
I try to get out,
In my mind
I scream and shout.
Someday I'll wake up
And then I'll know,
By that time it'll
Be my time to go.
In memories of sight
In memories of sound,
In memories of life
In memories I'll drown.

Jesse E. Reese

A BROTHER IS....

Someone who listens
Someone that's there,
To tell them anything
Someone to care.
Someone to trust
In any issue,
Ready to help
In anything upsetting you.
A friend for life
Through thick and thin,
Someone who'll go with you
On any path you begin.
Someone who's close
<u>*No matter how far apart,*</u>
A reliable person
For anything that may start.
Someone who loves you
And feels your pain,
Someone to bring you comfort
When you feel there's nothing to gain.
But most important
My brother are you,
Through life in it's full
Until eternity is through.

For my brother Robbie Reese.
May God watch over you and bring you home
Safely from Iraq and this terrible time of war.
Much Love,

Jesse E. Reese

A Lesson

The past is history
Which can not be changed,
The lessons to be learned
The life to be rearranged.
Once something is done
It becomes the past,
There to go by
Forever will last.
Remember what was
To change what will be.

Jesse E. Reese

<u>Being Alone</u>

Always searching
For what I don't know
Looking for answers
Direction to go
Lost and alone
Ready to quit
Forever in solitude
Here I will sit.

Jesse E. Reese

CHOICES IN LIFE

I said some things that I shouldn't have said
I've made you mad and very upset
All the things I have done
This is the one I regret.
I wish I could take back
The words I said
I wish you knew
What's in my head?
How much I love you
And want a life
With you beside me
As my wife.
I'd give anything for you
To be happy with me
Please forgive me
And accept my apology.
Without you I'm dead
I'm sorry it's true
My life doesn't exist
Unless it's with you.

Jesse E. Reese

Feelings

I wonder if this will ever end,
This feeling I have deep within.
A feeling of emptiness
A feeling of alone,
A feeling of separation
A feeling unknown.
For this is the feeling
I live with each day,
And I know it has decided
That it is going to stay.
In my mind
It's dark and hazy,
Twisting and turning
And driving me crazy.
I hope in the future
That someday I'll change,
Lighten and clear
My mind to rearrange.

Jesse E. Reese

For ?

Tingling in my stomach
Loss of appetite
Finally in my life
This feeling feels right,
In my thoughts
You are always
I never imagined
I would see these days,
Rejuvenated I now am
With happiness I almost forgot
To let this go
All I am will not,
A relationship has started
Between us two
My heart I give
Solely to you,
Hoping with you
My life will be
Full of joy,
Honest to you I promise completely.

Love,
Jesse E. Reese

If I Die

Would I be missed
If I would die,
Would anybody
Even cry?
I know people know me
But do they care?
I think I'm here
Just like air.
I know I'm here
But not seen,
To death
I am a feen.
Would I be missed
Would people know,
Would people care
Or just say, "so"?
Would people be happy
Or would they be blue,
There's one person that worries me
And that would be you.
Would you miss me
And be sad,
Or would you be happy
Joyous and glad?
I think it would be better
If I would die,
What would people do
Without a "good-bye".
I could go somewhere
And be on my own,
Somewhere quiet
And all alone.
A place away
From pain and hate,
I would sit
Alone and wait.
Wait for my day
To be in peace,
That only then
Will the page start to crease.

Jesse E. Reese

Insanity ?

About to collapse
I strain for fresh air,
Struggling for life
The amount of pain I can hardly bear.
Throughout my body
Is this intense feeling,
Inside my head
My ears are squealing.

Jesse E. Reese

My life

Spinning in out of control
My body shuts down,
Emotions are overflowing
As I begin to drown.
Losing all I am
Becoming what I'm not,
Trusting in dreams
My life I have forgot.
Chasing after love
In someone who I don't know,
Trying so hard
Not knowing which way to go.
I realize some things now.
Who was I kidding?
Out of my mind!
I'll continue to be alone
Love never to find.

Jesse E. Reese

New Beginning

So nervous
I can't see,
So many thoughts
Stampeding through me.
Don't know what to do
Or which way to go.
Feelings I have
Have been dormant for so long,
I wonder
If what I'm doing is wrong?
Standing breathless
I look at you,
Seeing my dreams
Without knowing what to do.
My heart starts to race
As I take a breath,
Finally my life
Is so far from death.
To see your smile
Your laughter to hear,
My dreams
My happiness, could be near.
Waiting for so long
On what is now,
I can't understand
Why or how.
I know that being with you
I feel something I thought was lost.
Searching my life
Without a clue,
I never thought
I would find you.
I'm forever in your debt
For what you've done,
From now
Until the end of the rising sun.

Jesse E. Reese

Perfidy

I sit outside in the fast
But gentle breeze,
Listening to the soft whispers
Of the voices of the leaves.
In the dark
With the winters wind,
My mind starts
To pretend.
What's real
And what's not?
I start to stare
In deep thought.
Things are moving
In ways they shouldn't be,
My mind is open
And running free.
The clouds are moving
In abstract ways,
Things have been strange
These past few days.
Shadows are dancing
All over the ground,
The wind, endlessly blowing
Is the only sound.
I'm all alone
With nature's grace,
Now my imagination
Starts to race.
I see colors
With trails of light,
What has happened
To my sense of sight?
I hear voices
In the back of my head,
They echo immensely
Unknowing what they said.
As my journey
Begins to end,
My mind surrenders to silence
Alone with myself, my one true friend.

Jesse E. Reese

<u>Relax to the sound</u>

I see without opening my eyes
I feel with closed hands,
I settle the conscience
As the sub-conscience demands.
Disconnected
To the world around,
Only feeling
Sight and sound.
The emotions are intoxicated
With the richness of vibrations,
The enticing atmosphere
The indulging of sensations.
Rhythm
The only guide,
It is all you have
On the other side.
In the place
Where conscience is not,
Music is all you need
Never a thought.
Once you get there
You are forever changed,
For all you've known
Has been rearranged.
Few people
Have reached the plain,
Where sound takes over
What the mind can't contain.
So close your eyes
Relax you mind,
Listen
And wait to find,
The part of you
That which was blind,
To the truth within
That has been confined.
The music of your Life.

Jesse E. Reese

Searching for Love

Looking for what I cannot find
Searching endlessly for what makes me be,
In the deepest corners of the minds imagination
Only to uncover the meaning of empty.
Forever wandering the vastness of time
Meandering about, waiting to stumble upon,
The missing part of life
I fear is now gone.
Suffocated by darkness
Blanketed by a hopelessness no one could know,
I'll diligently continue
For deep inside knows the direction to go.
Blindly I walk alone
The surroundings I feel,
Only through touch
I decipher what's real.
Trusting in something
I can't explain,
Forever searching
The relief if this pain.
From worlds unknown
Along the untraveled street,
Up the mountain with no name
And down the paths untouched be feet.
I've looked and searched
Through and through,
For a happiness
And a love I know to be true.

Jesse E. Reese

The End Is Here

The waiting
That I've done,
The passing of time
And settings of the Sun.
Purposeless days
And the empty nights,
All of the torment
The endless fights.
The never understanding by others
Of the memories carried,
The pain and the conflict
Will finally have a chance to be buried.
Erase the thoughts
Just inside my head,
Trying everything
Failing, I put to bed.
Overflowing heartache
The tearing in my chest,
The grinding of teeth
I now lay down to rest.
The endless headaches
The torturing past,
The transition after life
Will assuredly not be fast.
I say goodbye
For one last time,
With one more thought
To complete this rhyme.
When you feel
As something passed you by,
The love for you all
Will never die.

Jesse E. Reese

<u>The Game We Play</u>

Life is a game
That you play everyday,
As if someone controls
All you do and say.
Up until now
I've looked for peace,
Looked for the door
To make it all cease.
But now I've changed
I don't want out,
I want to stay in
To see what it's about.
To some people death
Is losing the game,
But to some others
Living's the same.

Jesse E. Reese

The pain of words

Thinking about tonight
And all that's been said,
Makes me wonder
If I'd be better off dead.
If the saying, "words can never hurt me"
Was actually true,
Then nothing would be said
Between me and you.
Sometimes people say things
They don't really mean,
But while they say them
The words are actually seen.
They can be seen in actions
And in the face,
It is hard to hide it
When emotions start to race.
There is another saying
"Actions speak louder than words"
That is a total lie,
Just one word can make a person die.
Not dying physically but emotionally.
It is much better to die physically
To be dead from life,
But being dead emotionally
You can still feel all the pain and strife.
To be dead and still living
Is torture unimaginable for any human,
It is like being alone outside
Knowing you cannot go in.

Jesse E. Reese

The Sun

I sit and watch the sun come to life.
Dancing it's light in this place we call home.
Starting it's magic we all call shadows.
Here and there and everywhere.
Causing life
Causing death,
But when we live
We are closer to dying with each new breath.
The sun is magnificent
In many ways,
Filling us with warmth and light
For all of these days.

Jesse E. Reese

This Feeling

Once again I feel this way
A feeling I've felt every day.
A feeling of sickness,
A feeling of death,
Yet a feeling of happiness
With every breath.
A feeling I missed
But always dread,
A feeling I thought
Was certainly dead.
I don't know why
I feel like I do,
Everything is so bright
But all so blue.
There could be many reasons
or just one,
A beautiful young light
As bright as the sun.
Even heaven
Can not amount to her smile,
It makes my mind race
Forever and a mile.
Maybe she's the reason
I feel like this,
The path is now clear
No way I could miss.
Wait! Who am I fooling
This can't be true,
I'll wake up, you'll see,
In a minute or two.
I'll never find happiness
No matter how hard I try,
I might as well quit,
Give up and die.
At least then
I'll be away from it all,
Away from life's
Vicious call.
So now I'll leave
With one last thought,
Don't ever fight this feeling
Whether you want to or not.
It will win
It's just too strong,
It doesn't care
If it's right or wrong.

Jesse E. Reese

TO BE A BROTHER

To always be there for any reason
Openly listen to any problems
A shoulder to lean on
A heart that is open
A bond unbreakable
A friendship without limits
Unconditional trust
Total honesty without fear
A life to give in a moments notice
Never forgetting who you are
Always with you no matter how far apart.

We are brothers
Let us never forget,
Willing to sacrifice
And ready to commit.
No matter the miles
That may lie between,
We are always there
Although unseen.
My brother you are
And always will be,
Brothers eternally
Robbie and Jesse.

Jesse E. Reese

TO MY MOMMY

Where to start
Let us see,
There is that
But that's not for me.
Ahead some time
As I grew inside,
The anticipation
I'm sure was hard to hide.
When I was born
For the first time you held me,
Laying there in your arms
Made me completely happy.
Diapers and formula
As the months keep going,
But what can I say
I am steadily growing.
I wake you up
At all hours of the night,
I know it's not fair
And even not right.
Sometimes to let you know
I have something to share,
But mostly to let you know
I love you and care.
I've tried you're patience
As I've learned and grown,
But your love for me
Is all that you've shown.
After a look at my life
I wanted to say,
I Love You Mommy and Thank You.
HAPPY MOTHER'S DAY!!!!!!!

Jesse E. Reese

Untitled

I know the road ahead will be rough
I know it will be pain,
To cover us both
And seem like a relentless rain.
I know it won't be easy
I know we will want to quit,
But we have to stay together
Each and every bit.
This is not an easy path
We chose to go down,
We may be alone
Like a dark dusty ghost town.
It will be a challenge
It will be Hell,
But no matter what
We can't crack like a bell.
We have to remain calm
No matter how hard it may seem,
We have to shine on everything
Like a powerful sunbeam.
All we will have to make this happen
Is the love we share,
The trust for each other
And the amount of care.
I will love you
Through thick and thin,
Through Heaven and Hell
And everything within.
I Love You.

With all my love from now till the end of
days,
We can make it as long as there is the love we share present.

Jesse E. Reese

<u>Visions</u>

I wonder why I am here?
I wonder what I need to do?
I keep wishing that the end is near.
I keep wishing my life were through.
I try so hard
With all my might,
Hoping someday
All will be right.
I shut my eyes
And close my ears,
Awaiting patiently
For what appears.
Visions of light
Visions of sound,
Visions of love
Visions of what I have not found.

Jesse E. Reese

VOWS

My life is complete with you standing there,
To love to care
Every breath to share.
A partner with you I'm willing be,
Through good though bad
Through all eternity.
By your side I'm forever here
Protecting you protecting your love
From doubt from pain from every fear.
I'll be your corner to which we'll build,
A lasting love a lasting happiness
That will forever be filled.
With our love hand in hand,
Together we'll face life
Together we will stand.
Through life through death together as one,
Nothing can harm
This life we have begun.

Jesse **E.** Reese

Walking Alone

The path I have found
Has taken me away,
From the things I know
And the words to say,
Leaving me here
Unsheltered and weary,
Standing alone
Where no one can see,
Looking back
Not knowing where I've been,
Tormented with the thought
Of where to begin,
Counting steps
I continue on,
Watching setting suns
How long I've been gone,
I find myself asleep
As day submits to night,
Dreams running free
Dancing in starlight,
Of what it would be like
To be over there,
Laying where it is warm
Where life comes without a care,
How happiness flows
Like an endless stream,
Then thunder crashes
Awake I am from that perfect dream,
Huddled alone
Weathering the storm,
Watching the lighting
The figures they form,
As the morning light
Peeks through the trees,
I rise from the ground
And get on my knees,
Collecting myself
As I look around,
The path that was there
Has been washed from the ground,
Myself I've lost
Now that I am here,
The emptiness overtook me
This being my greatest fear.

Jesse E. Reese

Made in the USA
Las Vegas, NV
20 November 2022

59898007R00015